A Casual Reconstruction / *Nadia Myre*

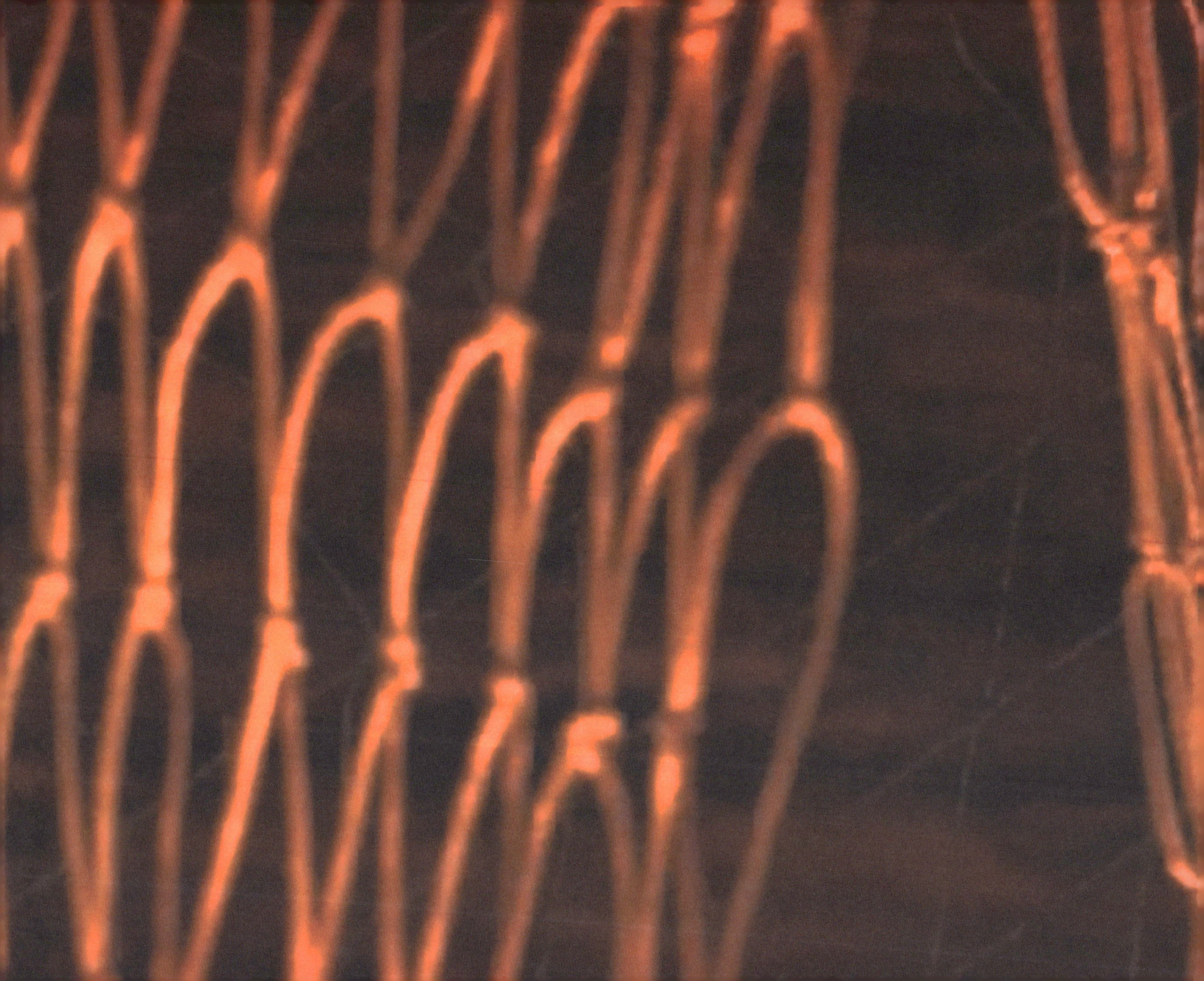

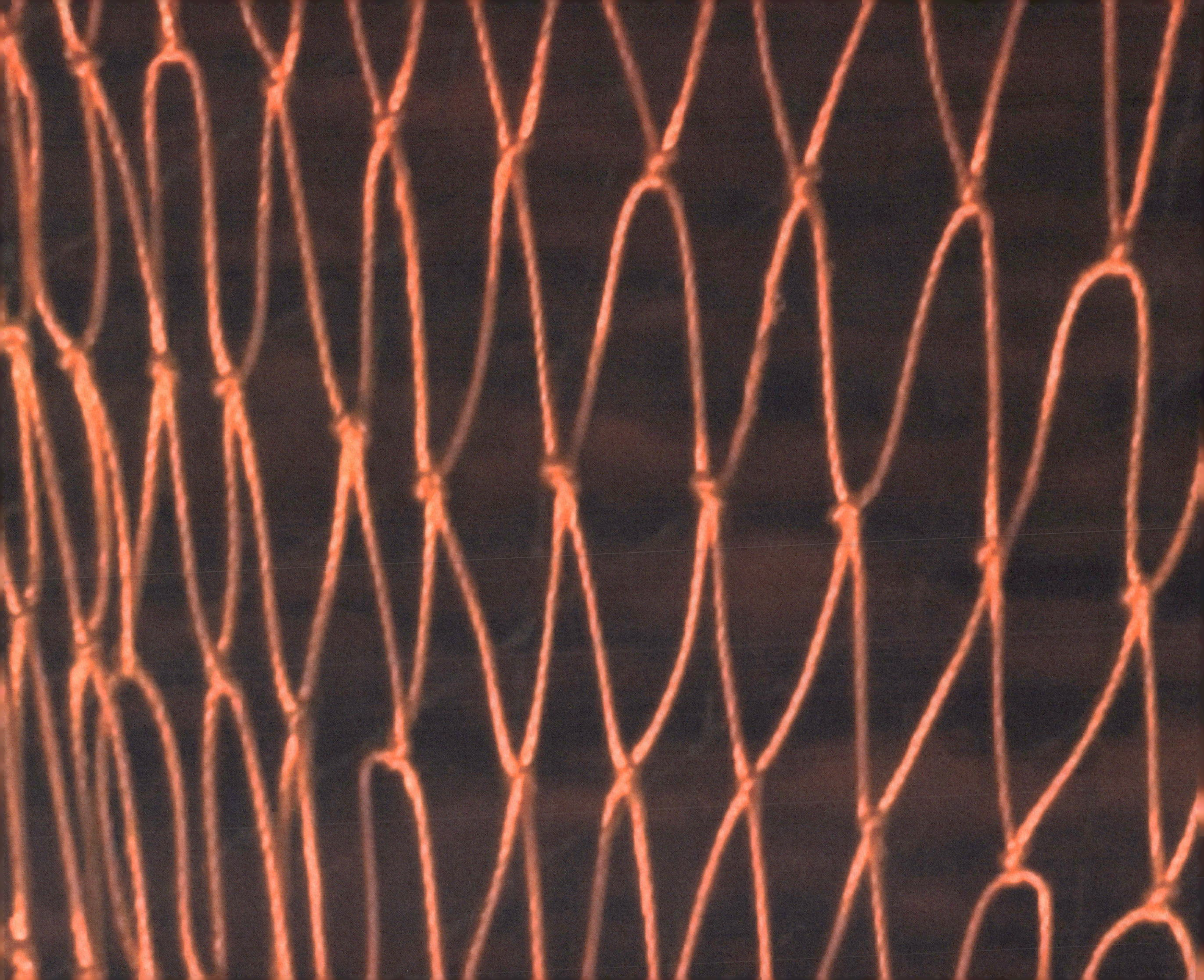

Foreword

A sense of belonging is a human need. It provides us with comfort, security and oneness. Without it one can feel isolated and alienated, unsure of the place where one fits. Our global society has created a vibrant hybridization of cultural identity and with it an underlying sense of social displacement.

A Casual Reconstruction explores open conversation to examine the relationship between language, identity and human connection. Driven by the desire to have an honest discussion about Indigenous identity/ mixed identity, artist Nadia Myre invites viewers on an intimate journey to probe the meaning of cultural distinctiveness. The interweaving of video projection and audio narratives serves as an intriguing rumination in understanding the meaning of belonging and the importance of the art of listening.

On behalf of the Robert Langen Art Gallery, I would like to express my sincere gratitude to Nadia Myre for her unwavering support and dedication to this exhibition and publication. A special thanks to award-winning author Louise Halfe for providing a poem that captures the emotions of Myre's installation and to Dr. Sara Matthews for contributing an essay that explores how social markers impact the notion of self. Thank you to our performers Nicholas Dinka, Christina Kerr, Robert Noecker, Sheldon Pereira, Deborah Wills and Anita Wei, who embraced their roles with great enthusiasm, and to Betty Winge for her creative wisdom and design expertise.

This publication was generously supported by the Ontario Arts Council. I would like to extend my thanks and appreciation for this financial support.

/ Suzanne Luke
CURATOR, ROBERT LANGEN ART GALLERY

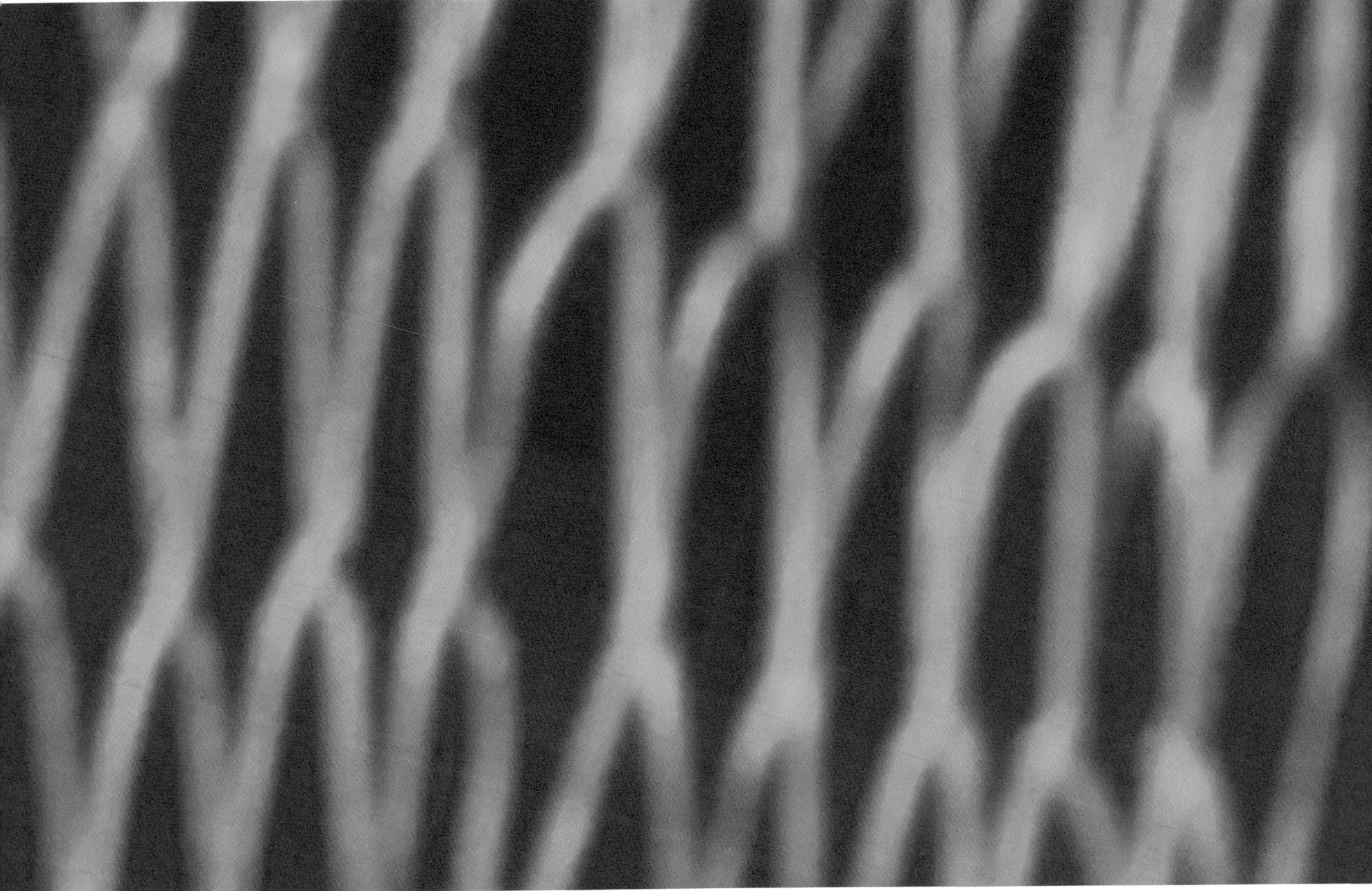

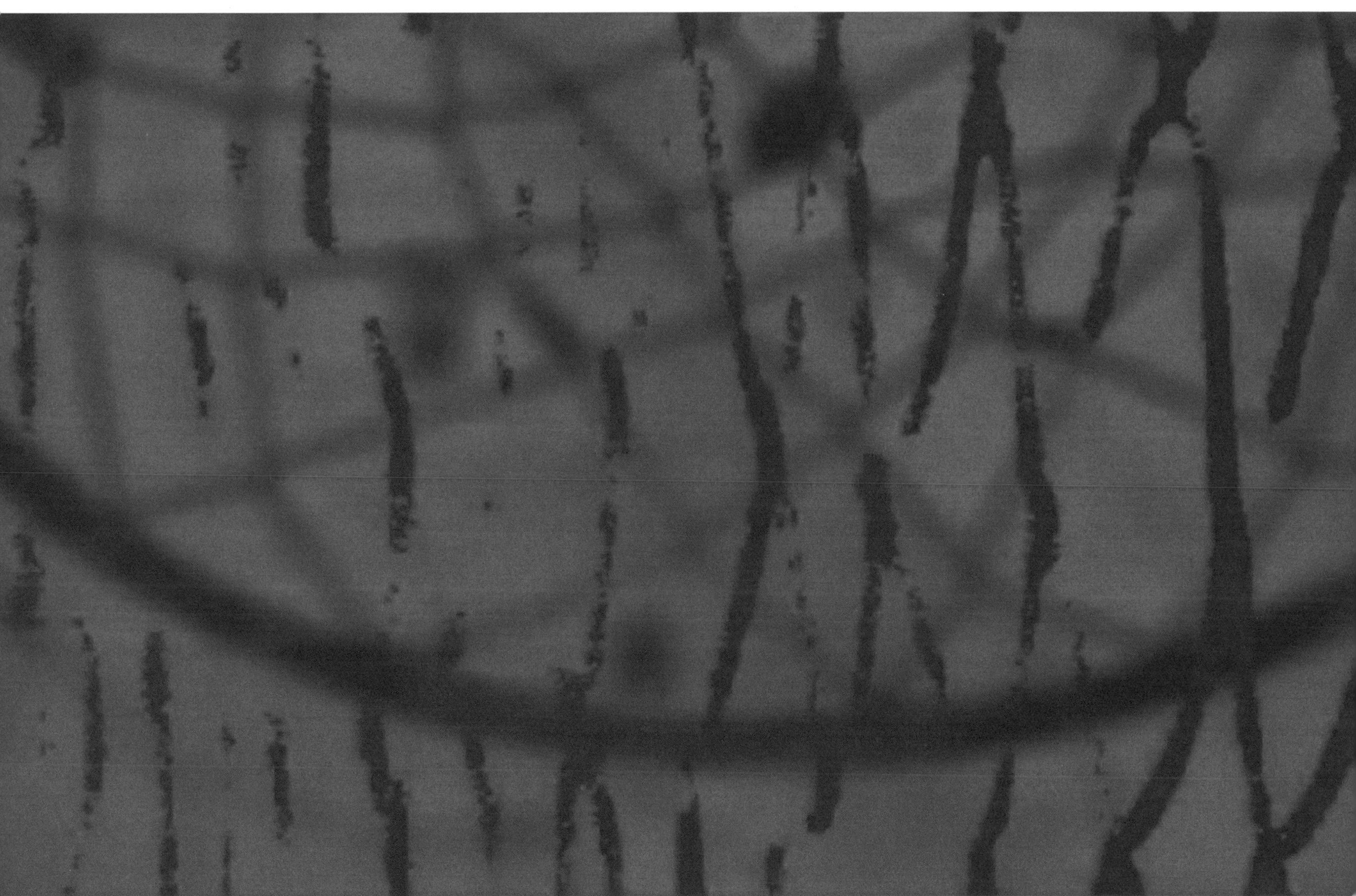

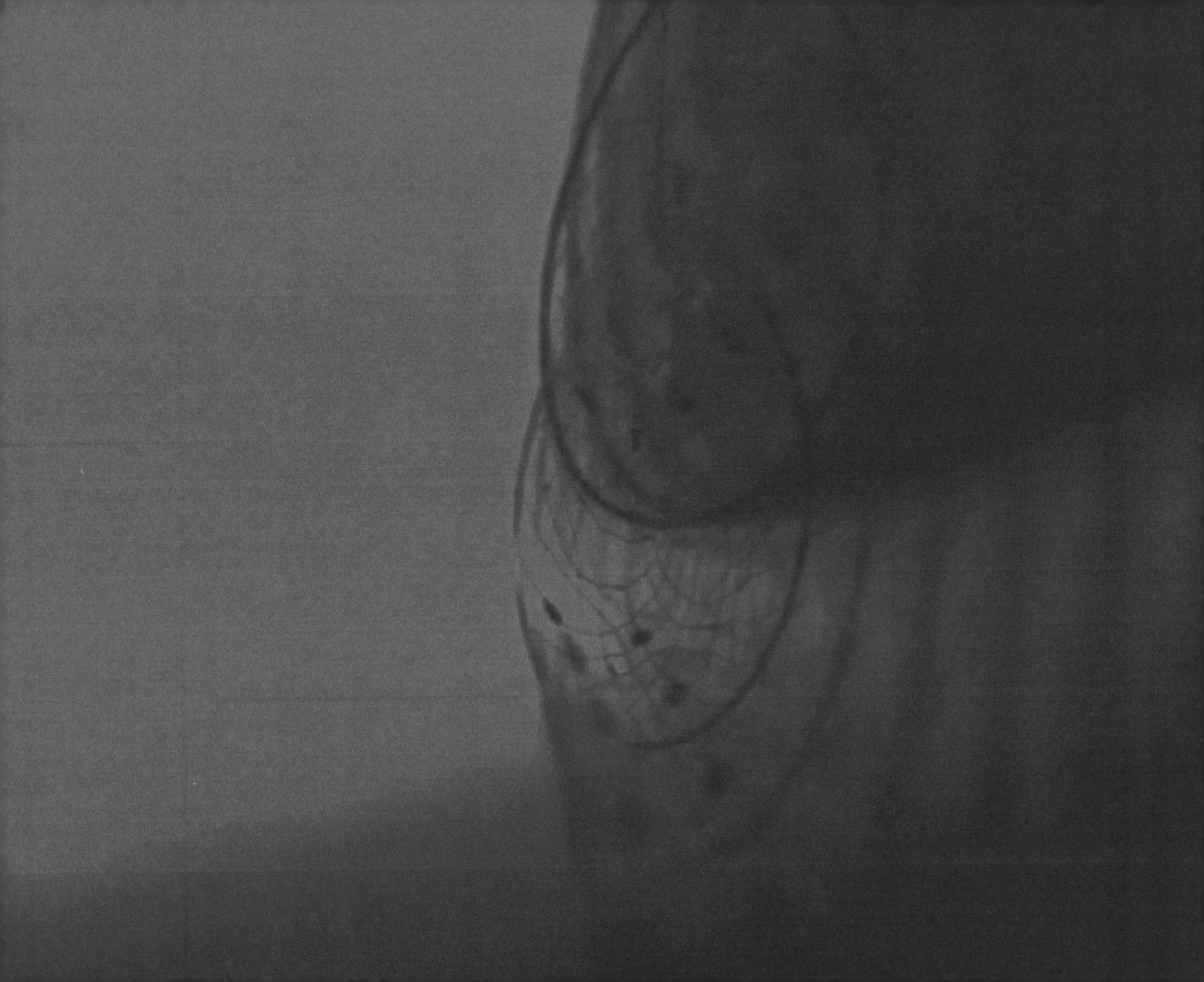

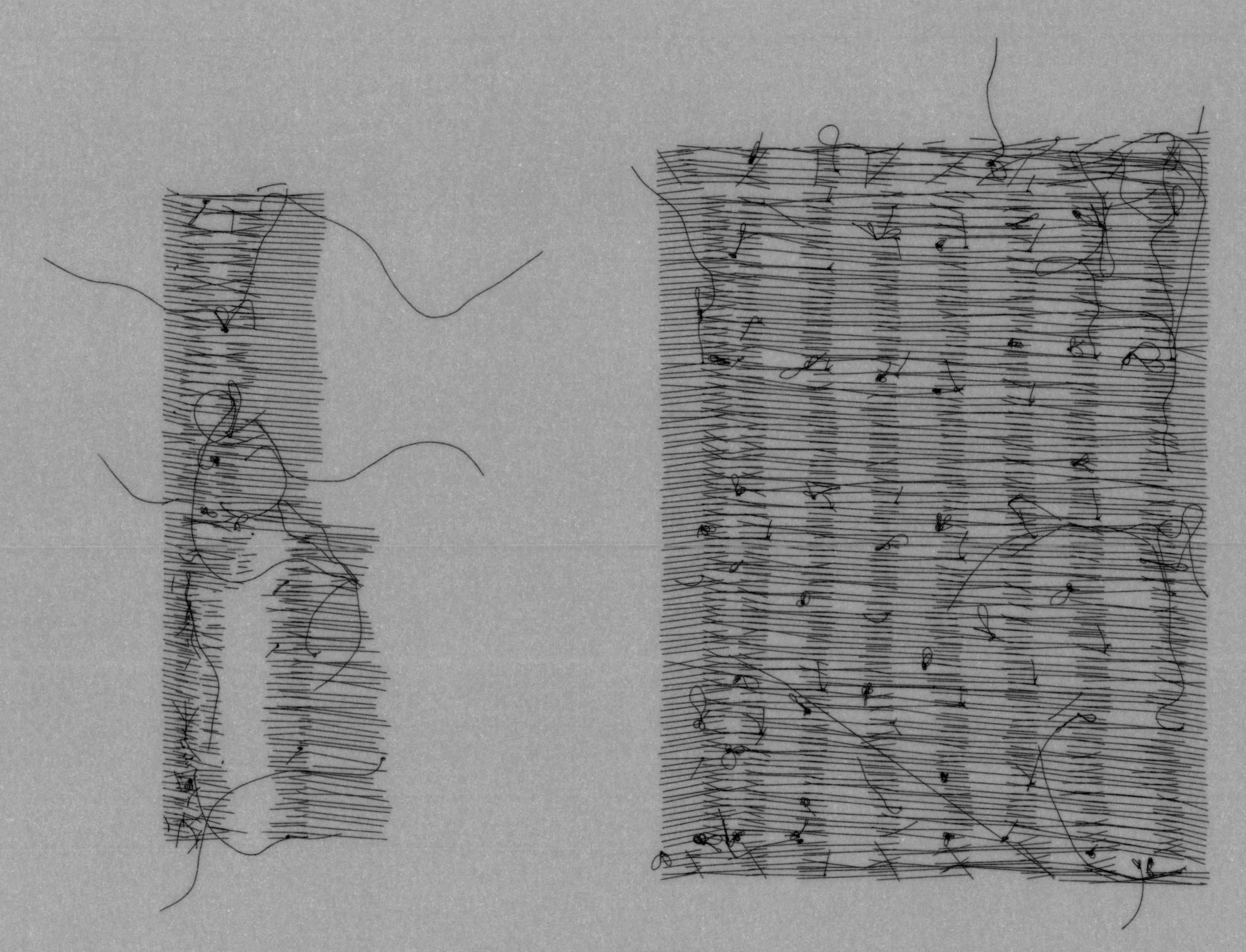

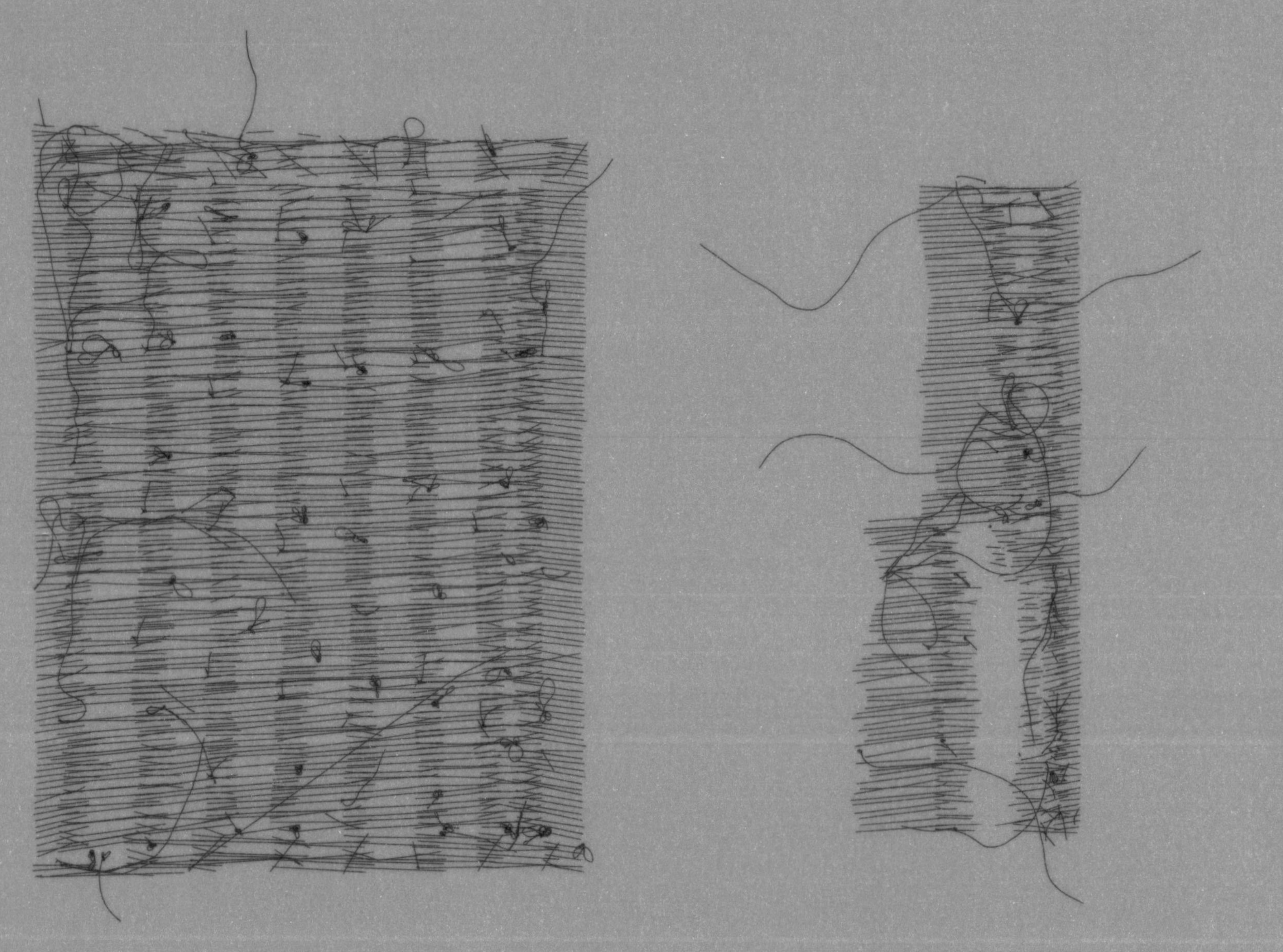

Wahkohtowin-kinship

In 1969 I attended my first Metis political gathering
And watched two burly men throw out a blond blued-eyed boy
As he cried
"I am an Indian. I am an Indian."
I was not to know that I too would become a grandmother
Of two blond blued-eyed grandsons
Whose hearts are those of the Cree
And another who is Black, Mi'kmaq and Cree.
When my half Cree and half Norwegian-British children
Where growing up I was repairing my soul, my spirit, my wind
From the ravages of residential school
From the scars of family malfunction.
I returned to the colonized reservation
Where I had buried my Cree heart
There I found my grandmother's sweat lodge
My grandfather's syllabics. I thought I had nothing to give
To my children until I went to these tents

And lifted the sweet grass, the sage and tobacco.
I am filled with trepidation for my grandchildren's generation
Whose bloodwater is that of the land, the wind, the fire.
They will be tracing their fingers
Along the genealogy of the tree
Where the smoke of the home fires may not welcome them
Because they didn't grow up on the trapline.
Wahkohtowin, we are all related
Yet the snare wire in the government's book
Has caught us like cattle upon this land.
We fight over who is Cree, Mi'kmaq, and Ojibwa
We fight over the pittance of money distributed for
Education, medical care, these treaty rights.
We categorize. We categorize. We categorize.
We are not wahkohtowin enough.

/ *Louise Halfe*

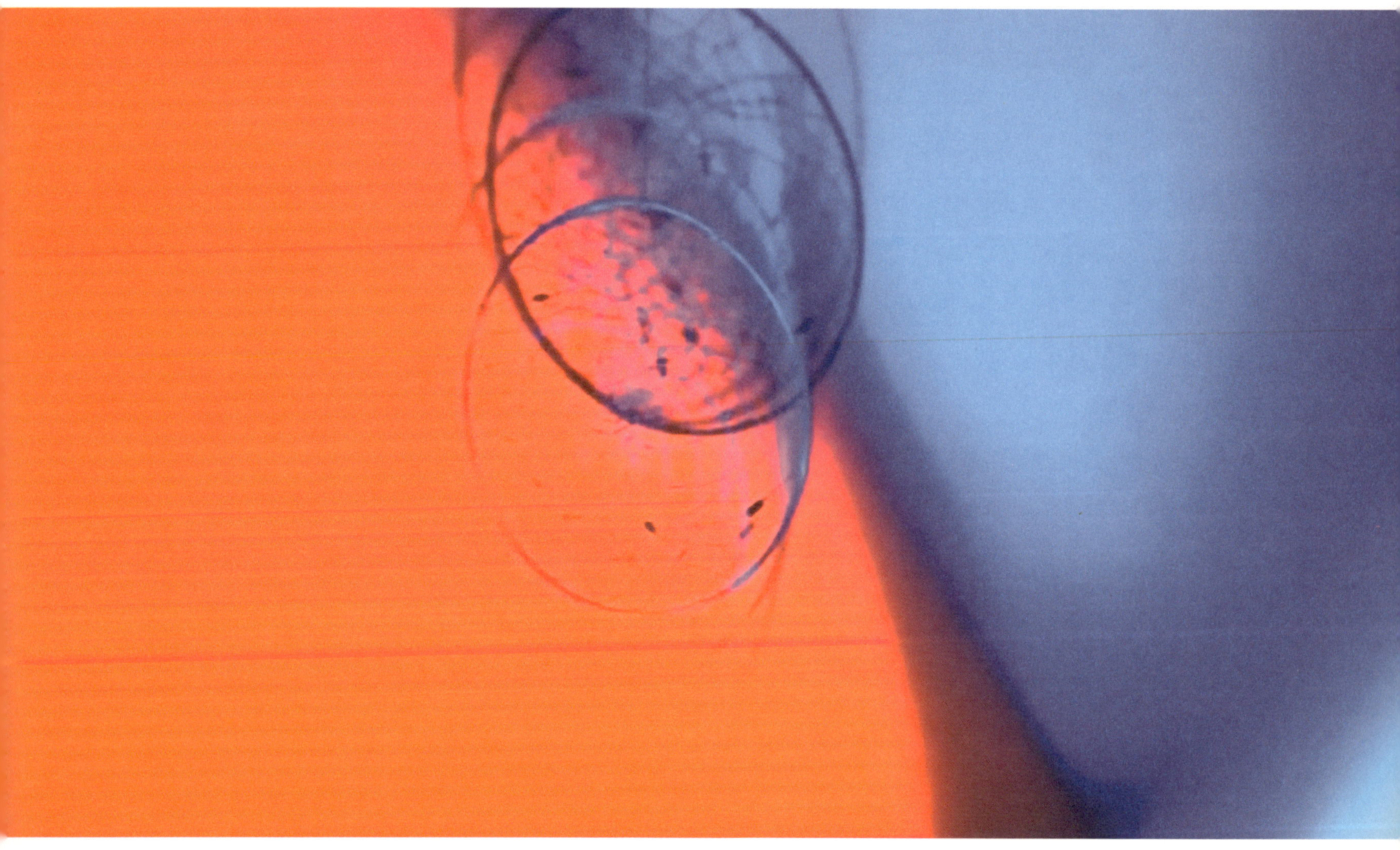

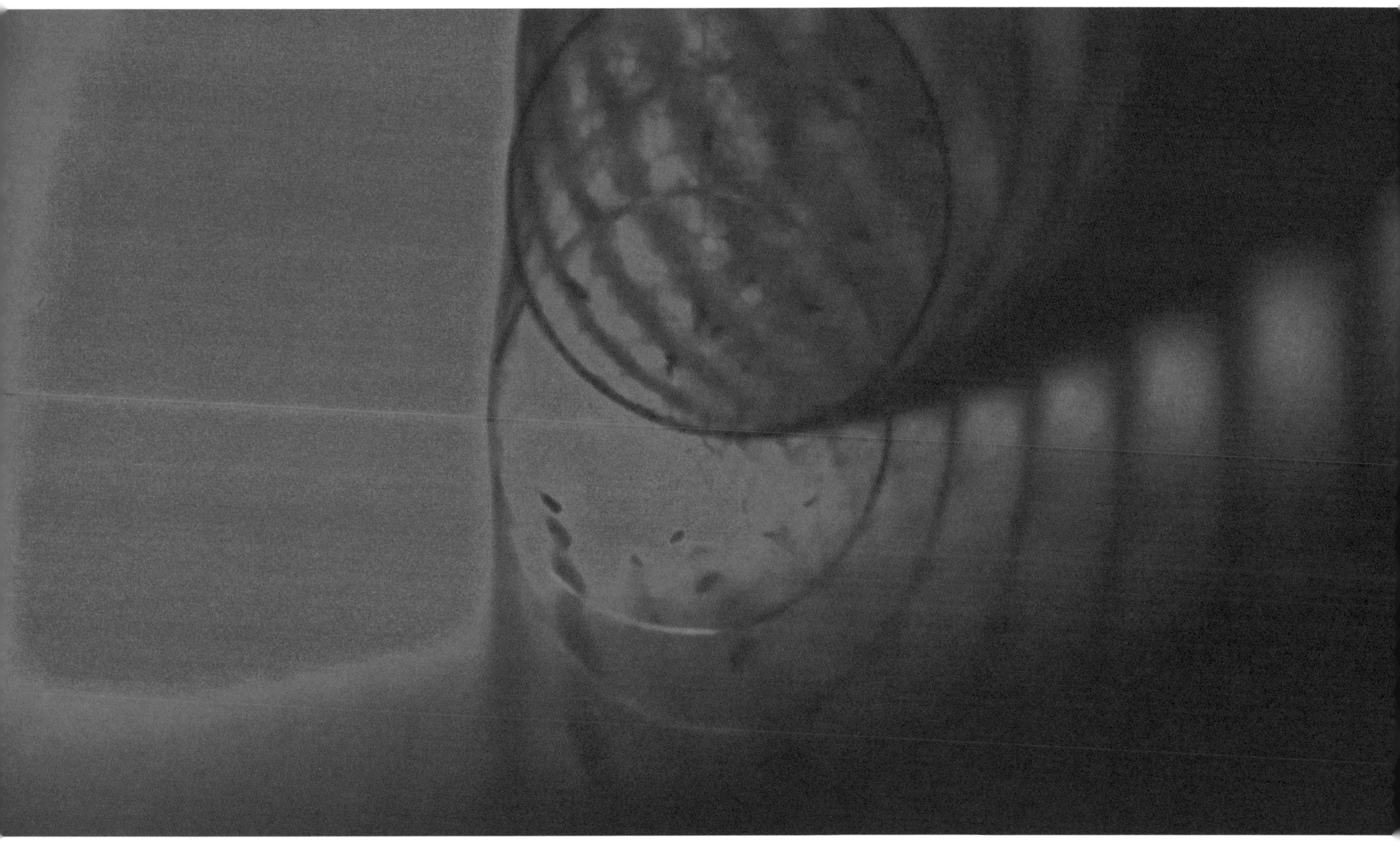

Proem

The inspiration for this work stemmed from a conversation I had with Miza'l Jeannotte Anglehart in New Richmond, Quebec[1] on August 29, 2015. Over lobster, he and I discussed identity markers as Québecois coming of age in the late 80's and early 90's: Mitsou, Nathalie Simard, Harmonium, Madonna, JoJo Savard, etc. At some point Miza'l said "Remember Janette Bertrand's *'Parler pour parler'*?" No...I didn't...How did I not know this? Pour temps, my father and I would sit in front of the TV, each in our lazy boy, watching whatever (French dubbed) Terminator, Jurassic Park, The Fly was showing on Radio-Canada or TVA. What was *'Parler pour parler'*? What other Québécois cultural markers had I missed? For the most part, I was raised by my dad, a proud Canadien Français, who at every opportunity corrected my french. How could my father have foreseen that his effort towards my fluency would widen our cultural rift? That in reaction to this language wound, I would chose to be the Anglophone in a French speaking family; the Algonquin in a Québécois one? Or that I would sooner piece together a culture and family I never knew (my mother's), and claim it, than to continue to feel incompetent in one I grew up with. At some point during dinner I said to Miza'l "For me, identity is an active choice", to which he disagreed. *A Casual Reconstruction* was born from the desire to have an honest discussion about identity and mixed identity as Indigenous people and stage my own *'Parler pour parler'*.

This work is a fruit which continues to ripen through the act of many collaborative exchanges. This piece would not have come into being without Miza'l Jeannotte Anglehart (and our dinner guests: Mary-Jane Condo, Cindy Condo, Chris Brasier and Josh Philbrick). I am equally thankful to Marie Novack from Vaste et Vague for recording the original conversation, and to Brian Gardiner, for shaping it into a 30 minute piece and transcribing our words verbatim. Translation of this text to french was provided by Benoit Trépanier and Anne-Marie Proulx, the English edit was revised by Lib Spry.

/ Nadia Myre

[1] The name "Quebec" comes from a Mi'kmaq word k'webeq meaning "where the waters get narrow" and originally referred to the area around Quebec City, where the Saint Lawrence River narrows to a cliff-lined gap. French explorer Samuel de Champlain chose this name in 1608 for the colonial outpost he would use as the administrative seat for the French colony of Canada and New France.

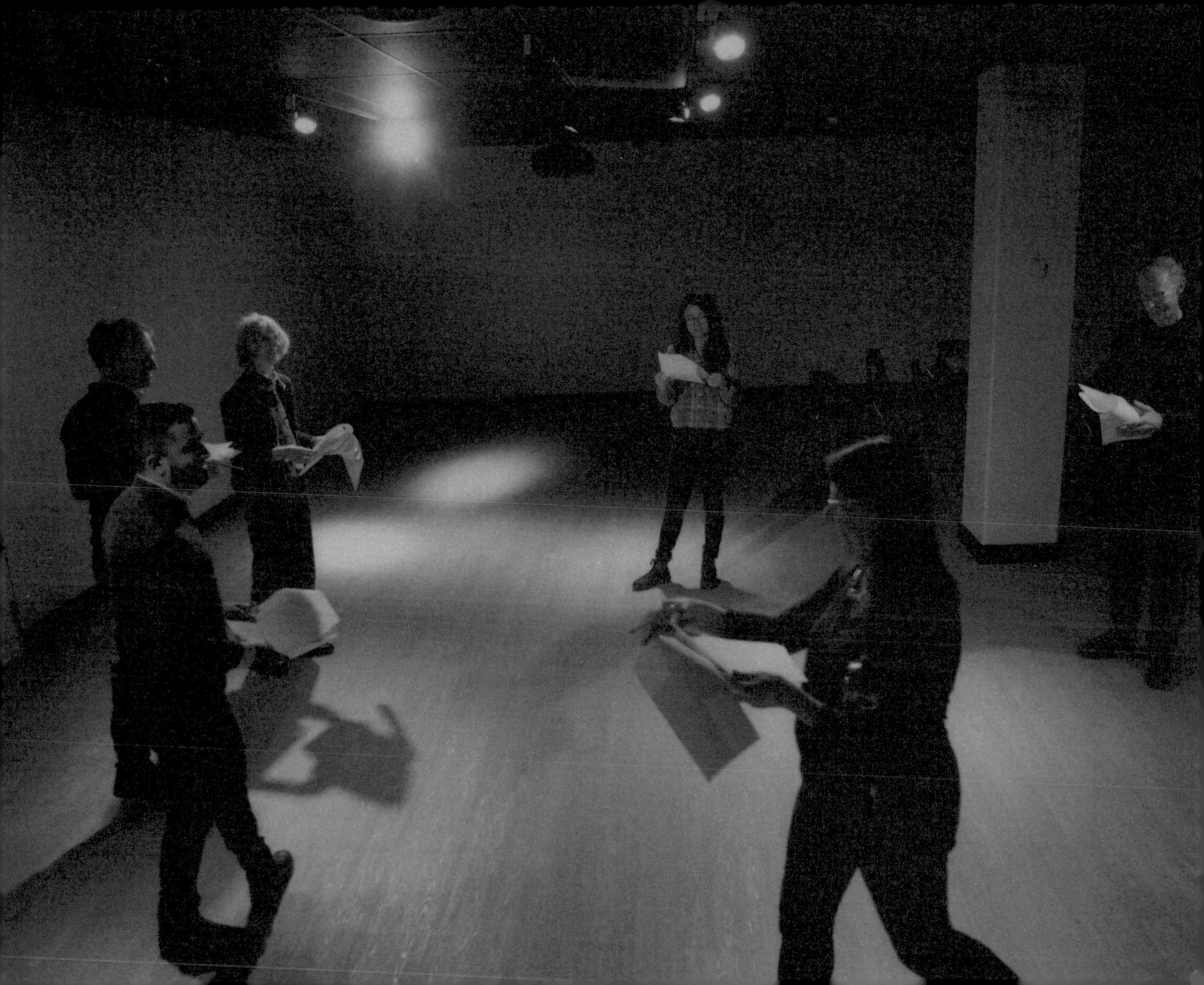

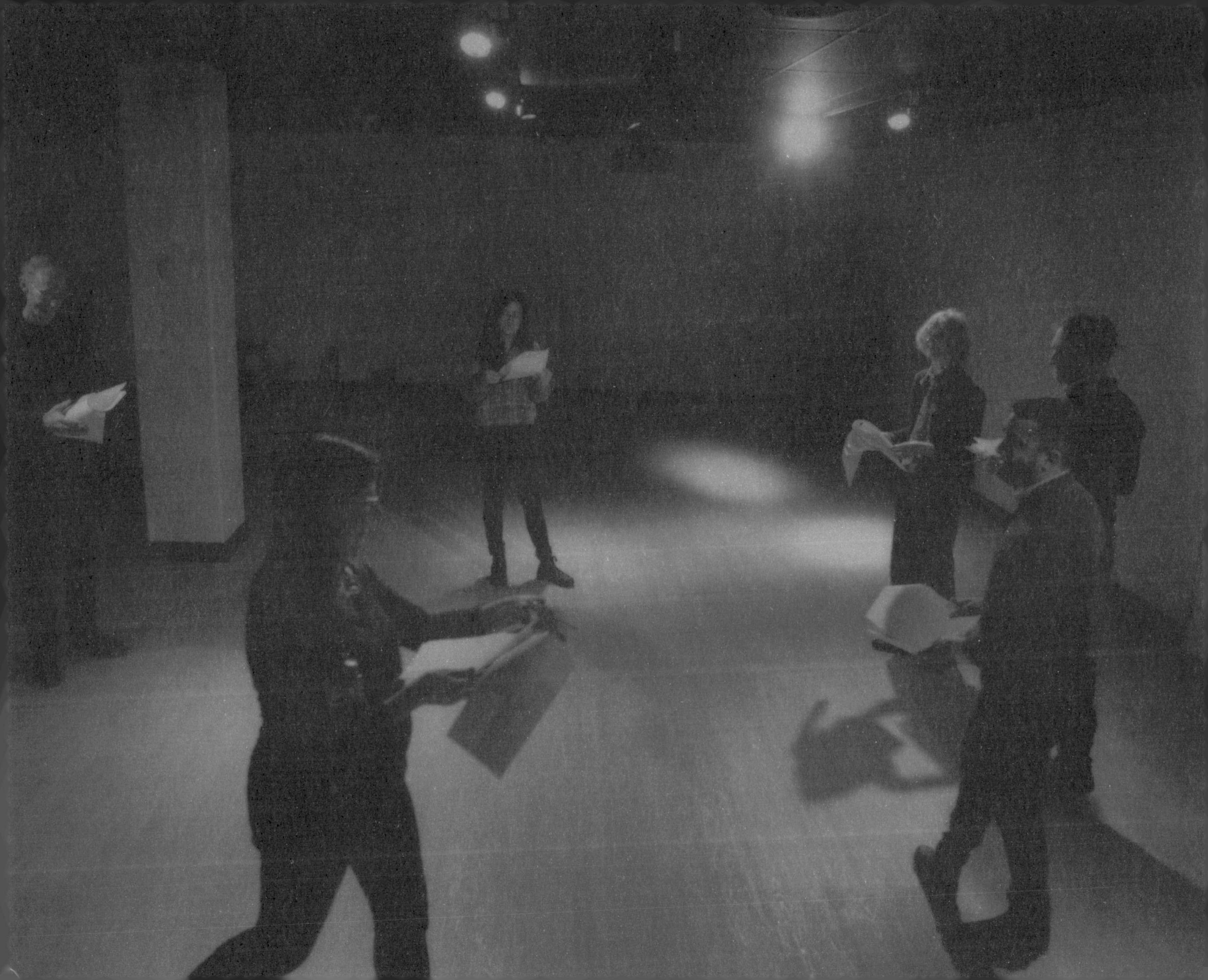

Reconstruction *as* Relation / *Sara Matthews*

"Our objective is to continue until there is not a single Indian in Canada that has not been absorbed into the body politic and there is no Indian question, and no Indian Department"

DUNCAN CAMPBELL SCOTT, DEPUTY MINISTER OF INDIAN AFFAIRS (1920)

MIZA'L   *"Le coté patriarcal is a white way"*

JOSH   *"Yeah"*

MIZA'L   *"Because that's what the government did"*

JOSH   *"Yeah"*

MIZA'L   *"It was all...the purpose was to eliminate as much Native people"*

JOSH   *"Yeah, yeah"*

MIZA'L   *"So because women bear children, if you go out and marry white you're not an Indian anymore, so your children"...*

CINDY   *(cutting in) "Back then is if you were non Native and you married Native you got your rights now Natives can't get their rights"*

JOSH   *"Yeah"*

MIZA'L   *(cutting in) "Yeah, the men. This was the intention, to eliminate so many generations"*

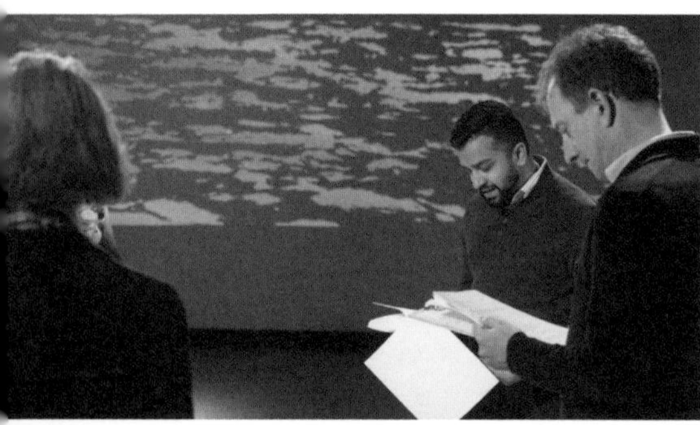

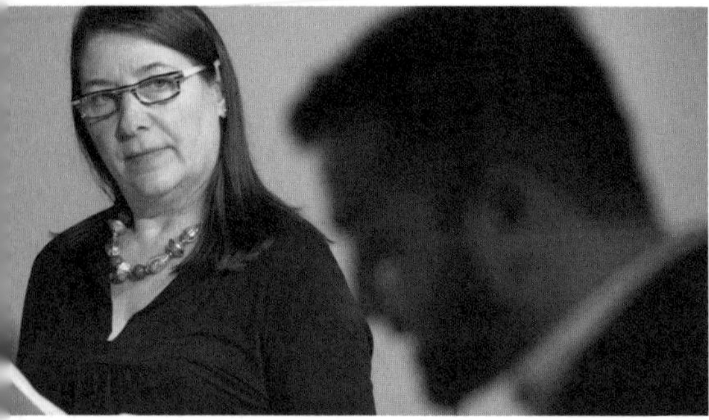

Nadia Myre's multi-media installation *A Casual Reconstruction* (2015) is a collaborative work that documents and recreates a dinner conversation between the artist and several of her peers who, over the course of a shared meal, candidly express their thoughts and feelings about what it means to survive the enduring legacies of Canada's assimilationist policies and to find belonging as mixed-race Indigenous people. A founding premise of the settler colonial nation now known as Canada, assimilation was orchestrated through carefully constructed legislative policies and social practices that aimed to alienate Indigenous communities from their lands, rights, social relationships, families, structures of governance, languages and cultures. With her video installation *A Casual Reconstruction*, Myre harnesses the spontaneity of dinner table dialogue to animate the formalized effects of settler colonialism as a question of relation – to the self, to language, to community and to place. Documented verbatim from the original dialogue and edited into a 30-minute digital projection, the video invites the listener to eavesdrop on that conversation. At the opening of the installation in a gallery setting, it has been Myre's practice to invite non-Indigenous participants to perform a scripted reading of the work. I was present for just such a reading at Robert Langen Gallery on March 8, 2017.

The term "casual" brings to mind an informality, a shared sense of ease and social intimacy. As a reconstructed conversation, the reading of the dinner dialogue by non-Indigenous participants plays with the notion of familiarity, staging difference while inviting identification between the performer and their 'character', and also between the viewer and the dinner guests whose words the performers are speaking. If conversation can be thought of as an attempt to create, through verbal exchange, a space for understanding the self in relation to others and the larger social world, then the space made by *A Casual Reconstruction* is one of intimate relation to the dialogue that Myre sets in motion.

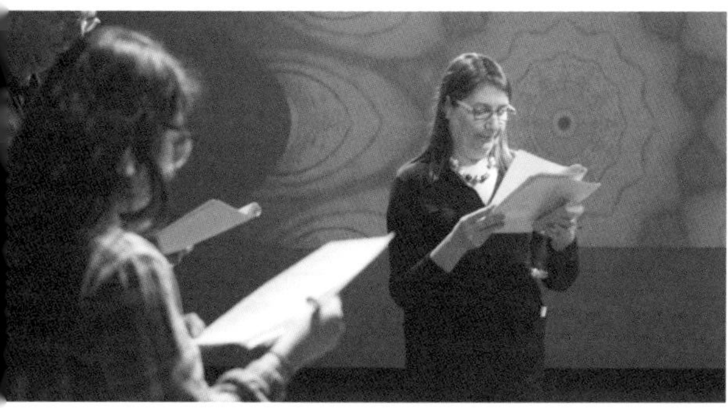

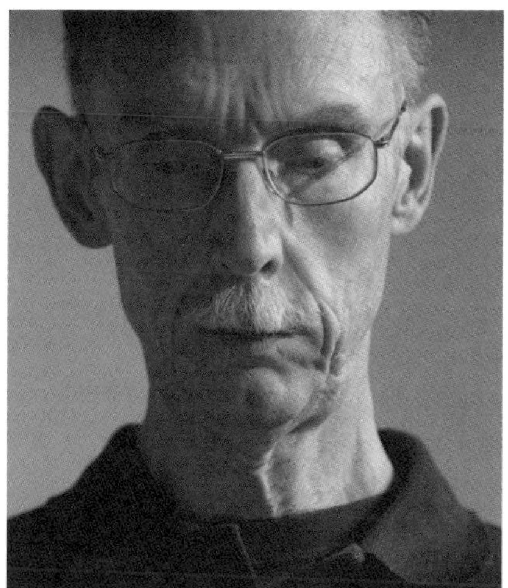

On opening night, the gallery was configured to promote this kind of amity by the arrangement of seating in a large horseshoe surrounding an inner circle. I chose a seat in that inner ring, sitting with five other gallery goers waiting for the reading to begin. Six performers, each adopting a speaking role from the original group of dinner participants, moved into standing position behind our chairs. This proximity interrupted the typical viewing dynamic that separates audience from art and artist. As the performers read their scripted roles, circling the chairs in distinct movements or "acts", something curious occurred: words, language, affect, and movement worked in concert to catalyze a space of opening and implication. A reconstruction is an iteration that involves repetition, but repetition with a difference. In the gap between the original dinner conversation and its animation, room for relation, spontaneity and dialogue is provoked. After the performance I had a chance to connect with the individuals who participated in the scripted reading and learned that they too, were surprised by the ways in which the reading called them into dialogue – both with the histories of assimilation to which Myre's piece speaks, and with their own stories of coming to know themselves in relation to contemporary resonances of that history. I have captured some of those thoughts, with their permission, below. *A Casual Reconstruction* is an iteration of an original, but also the construction of something new - a relation to what one does not yet know about one's implication in the violent legacies of nation building that we all share.

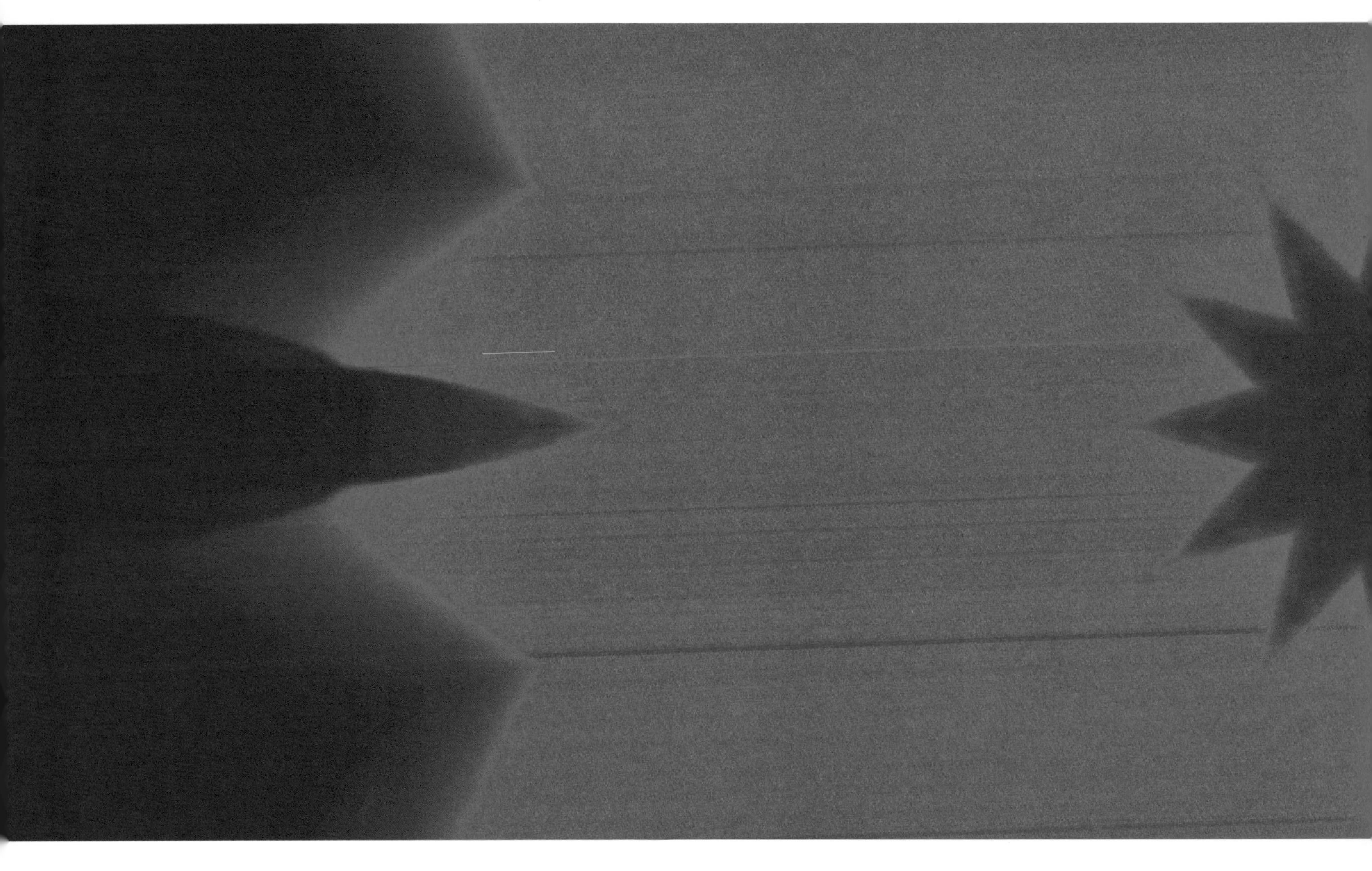

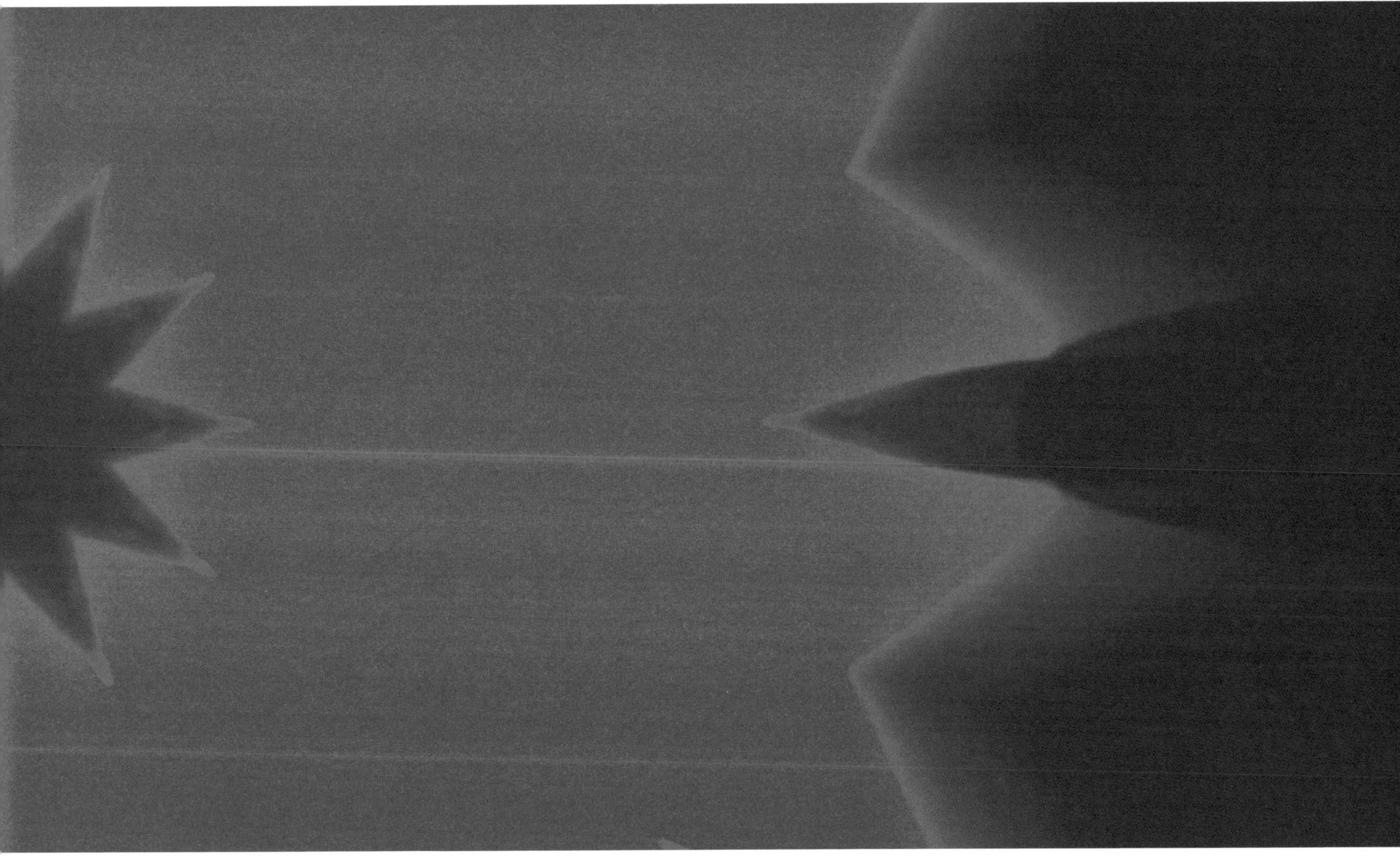

The day before the performance, Nadia assigned us our character. As I read the character script, I couldn't help but worry about delivering the script with the authentic voice that it deserved. The script was woven with notions of identity - whether Indigenous, Francophone, or gendered - and I wanted to convey the character in a way that was fitting and true. To whatever extent that may have been possible.

My chief concern was to pronounce the Mi'gmaq words and phrases correctly. I didn't want to offend anyone. I wanted to present the individual I was reading for as honestly as possible.

I have zero acting experience and was worried I would be terrible.

My concerns around reading my character's words with an authentic voice were calmed, almost immediately, as I came to realize the congruence between my past and present crises of identity, and that of the character's. There was a certain comfort, as strange as that sounds, with the struggle of my character to find his place and his identity, growing up. Similarly, albeit in a different context, I went through cycles of struggle, tension, and hybridization as I tried to fit in. See, my family immigrated to Canada when I was a young boy. And I wasn't entirely Canadian to my new friends, nor was I entirely local when we visited home either. I was caught between worlds, I suppose. And sometimes in my effort to fit in, I would blend both identities instead of adopting one or the other. Sometimes by choice, and other times, by accident. In reading my character's words, I was taken back to many moments in my youth. And his reflections on being native and fitting in, felt comfortable to me, even though the lived experience wasn't my own. I couldn't possibly understand what it might have been like to live his life, but I certainly found empathy within myself for how he might be feeling through the dinner party.

So I am a "white guy" and I think this led to interesting mixed feelings. On the one hand I enjoyed the process and found myself getting into it. But at the same time there was a voice in the back of my mind worrying about voice appropriation and my right to take on this person's voice. In the end I think it made for some interesting reflections on the nature of identity and difference. I like to think it brought me closer in a however imperfect way to getting a sense of this Aboriginal man's perspective.

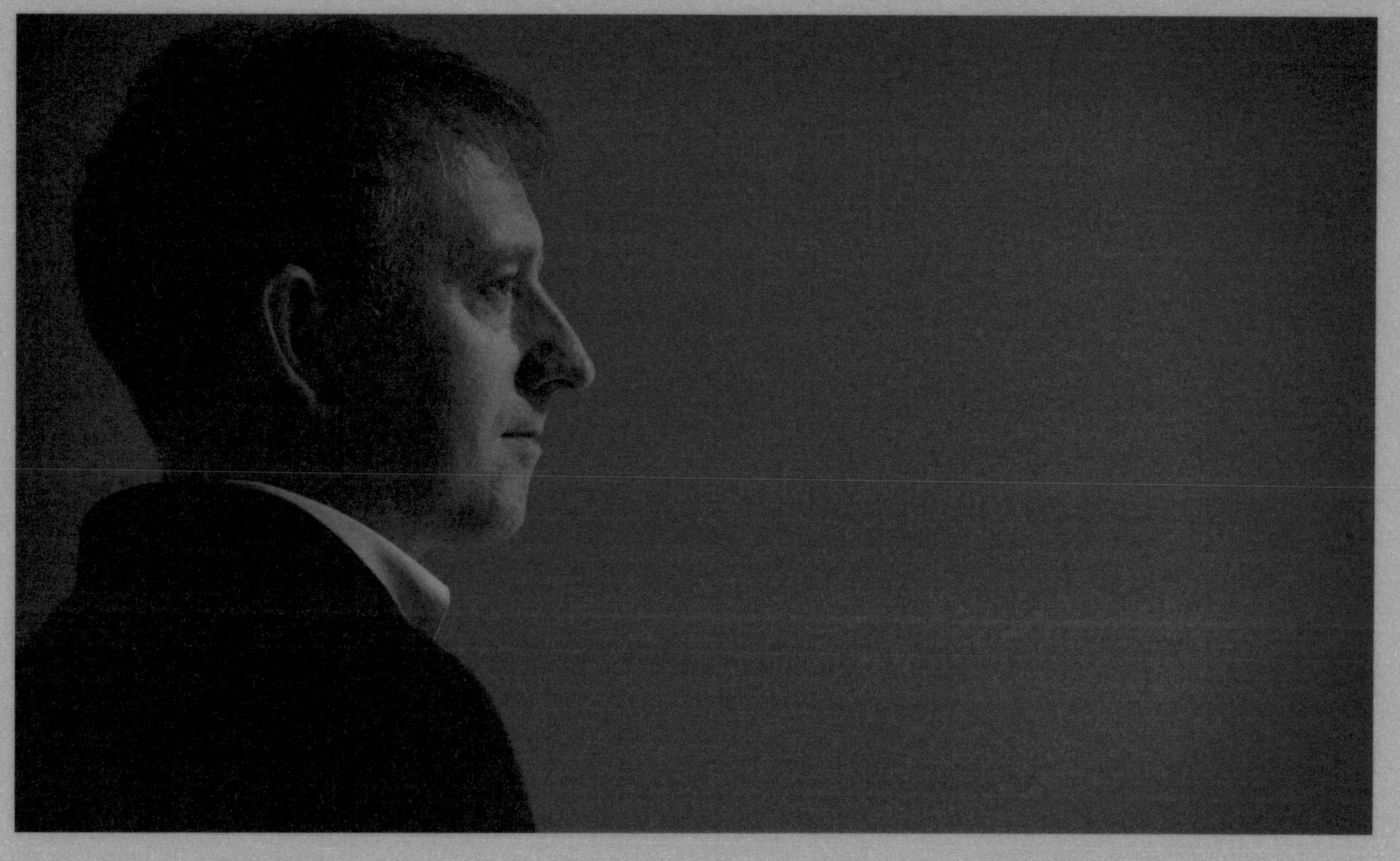

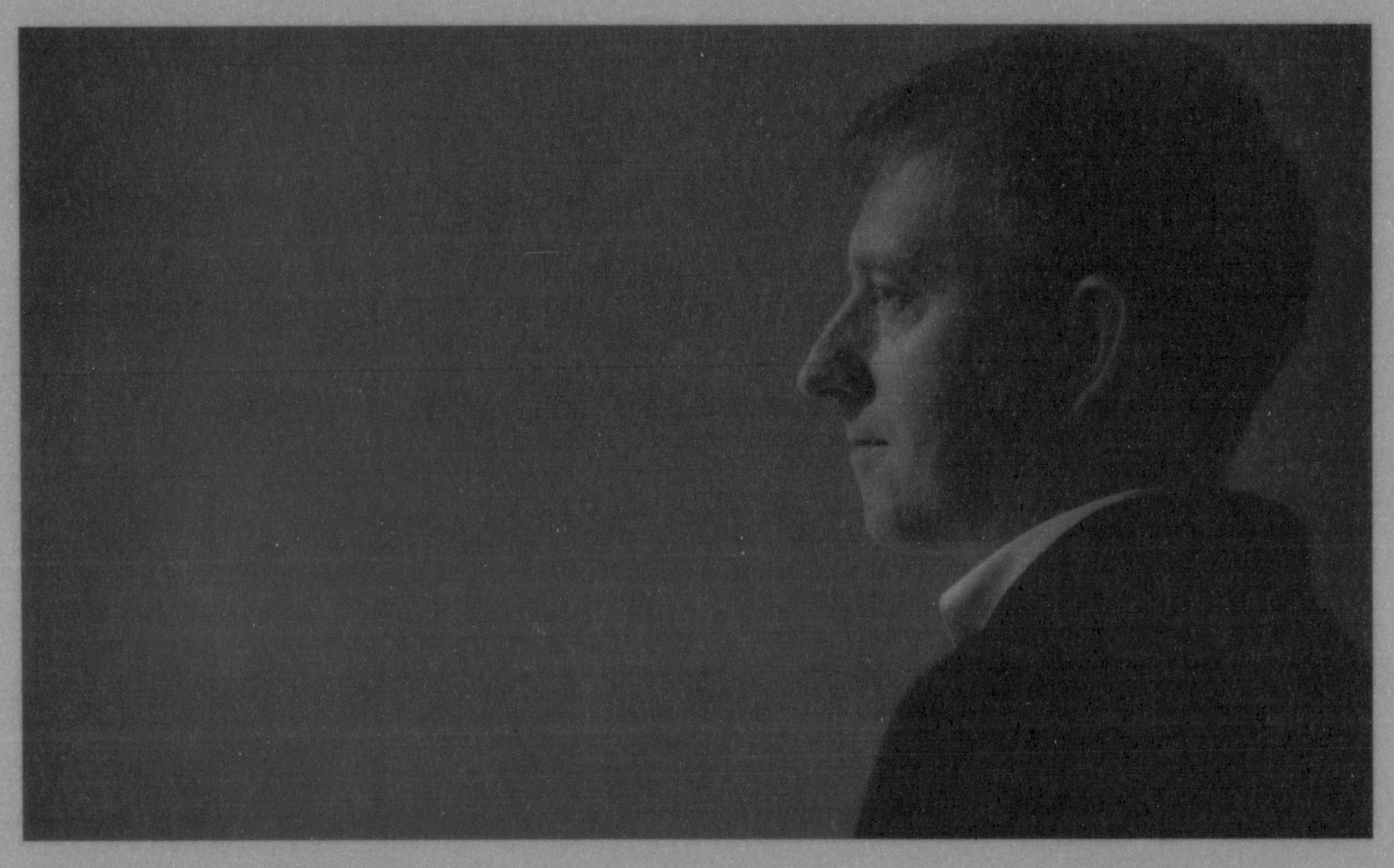

My part resonated with my own experience. [My character] doesn't know a lot about Aboriginal language. She can understand a little bit, but has difficulty in speaking. Her mother strongly insisted in letting her grandchildren learn the language from school. This scenario reminded me of Chinese immigrants: my boyfriend is Canadian-born Chinese. His parents are both Chinese native speakers, and they talk in Chinese at home. But my boyfriend uses English as his first language and hardly speaks Chinese at home. Imagine this scenario: his parents speak in Chinese – he responds to them in English. What a weird conversation. And my boyfriend told me many times: you gotta teach our kids Chinese. You need to let them know Chinese culture, poetry, and history, and I wanna learn together with them.

As I read the words, my character became more real for me. Although his life and concerns are different from my own, his points of view, regarding identity and language, were understandable.

As different as we all are, each of us wants to know who we are and how we fit into society.

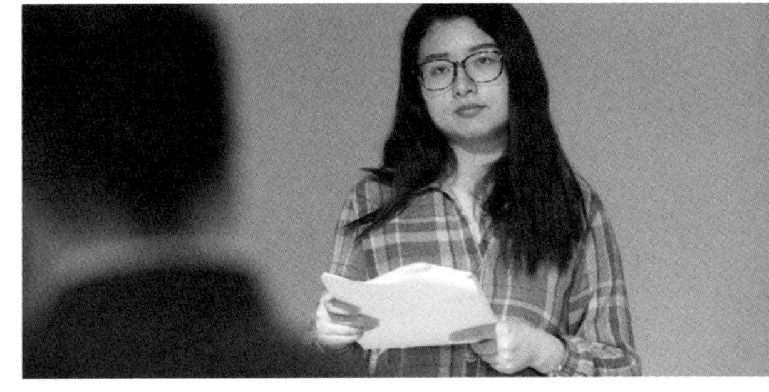

Now, as I reflect back, I have mixed feelings on my life and the performance. There are times where I am eager to dive into conversations of identity. And other times, I tire easily -- because sometimes, it's not entirely comfortable or comforting to be reminded through these conversations that you are the "other". When really, sometimes, you just want to be native. Which I suppose, is the irony. So many of our native brothers and sisters are made to feel like the outsiders, when in fact, we're the ones visiting Turtle Island.

i. National Archives of Canada, Record Group 10, volume 6810, file 470-2-3, volume 7, pp. 55 (L-3) and 63 (N-3).
ii. Nadia Myre, A Casual Reconstruction, script (2015). By permission of the artist.
iii. http://www.nadiamyre.net/work/#/a-casual-reconstruction-gallery-version/ retrieved April 16, 2017
iv. Canada, Georges Erasmus, and René Dussault. 1996. Report of the Royal Commission on Aboriginal Peoples. Ottawa: The Commission.

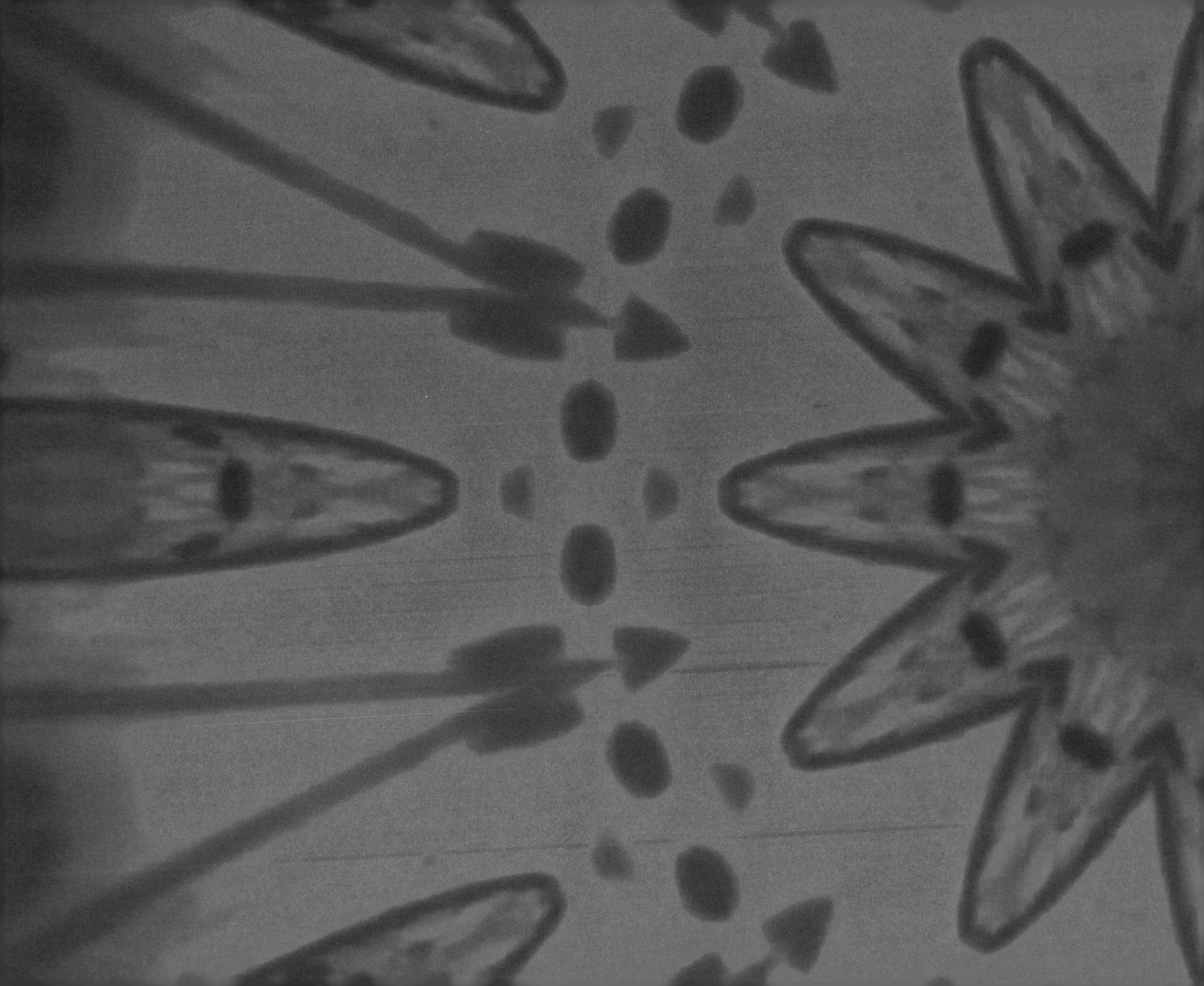